My Frontliner Mother's, Mother's Day Everyday

Author:	Chantal V. Magracia - Ouldzini
Editor:	Sam Wright
Illustrator:	Aiwaz Jilani
Arabic Translator:	Suzan Nihad
French Translator:	Leticia Stalling

First published in Canada in 2020 by Chantal Magracia.
Copyright © 2020 Chantal Magracia
ISBN: 978 - 1 - 7772044 - 0 - 2

FREE DOWNLOADABLE WORKSHEETS

TEACHERS & PARENTS,
If you would like to access the worksheets for this specific book:
1. Please go to my website: philmorcan.com
2. The worksheets would be under the heading "FREE DOWNLOADS".

philmorcan.com
philmorcan@gmail.com
facebook.com/philmorcan
instagram.com/philmorcan
youtube.com = subscribe to "PhilMorCan"
Amazon.ca = search for "Chantal Magracia"

DEDICATION

I would like to dedicate this gift to my beloved mother, Ludy Magracia, my mother-in-law, Fatima Ouahdani, the best auntie, Analiza Villavicencio, and my soul sisters, Nina Diaz & Suzan Nihad, for their consistent and constant display of uncomparable and unconditional love.

To Dr. Deena Hinshaw,
the frontliner hero during the COVID-19 pandemic in Alberta, Canada, who saved countless valuable lives.

To all the frontliners & essential workers who continuously risk their health and safety for the sake of their fellow countrymen, we salute you all for your courage, bravery, and generosity with your time, skills, and talent.
Frontliners and essential workers including all healthcare workers, emergency service workers, police officers, firefighters, military personnel, social workers, teachers, bank personnel, truckers, transportation workers, delivery drivers, supermarket staff, fast food and restaurant staff, gas station clerks, electricity and water staff, janitors, journalists, politicians, government workers, court staff, religious personnel, prison and probation officers -- from the bottom of our hearts, we sincerely and deeply thank you for all of the hard work and efforts that you put forth daily.

*Last, but not least, I dedicate my work to all mothers who always do their best for their children and who always prioritizes their families first.

*Likewise, I also dedicate this work to all children who always do their utmost best to put their mothers first by showering them with love, care, affection, and appreciation. Make your mothers proud.

Live, Laugh, Love, & Light,
Chantal V. Magracia - Ouldzini a.k.a. "Selma"

What Are You Grateful For?

It was a warm and sunny Monday morning, my brain was groggy and my body felt unsteady because I was still half-asleep, when Ms. Villavicencio quietly placed a worksheet on my desk.

I briefly glanced at it, and the title asked, "What Are You Grateful For?"

It was such a simple question, but it struck me right in my core because I had a lot of thoughts, emotions, and feelings about this question. Yes, feelings! I had to shake myself to wakefulness as it was time to put myself to work.

As my mother always taught me, "There is always a right time and a right place for everything, Arabella. Manage your time productively, and you will go far in life with everything you do. The more you do now, the less you'll have to do later … which means you'll have more time to enjoy life eventually."

Of course, I only understood my mom's words half of the time, and the other half still requires me to reflect upon them, and hopefully, my brain will be able to completely absorb the 'epiphanies' she wants me to discover and learn…

… which brings me back to the question right before me. It made me really think about the answers -- long, deep, and hard. I thought to myself, 'What is it exactly that I'm thankful for?'

I knew the answers right off the bat! It didn't even take me THAT long to know the answers in my heart. I mean, come on! It was a no-brainer!

I began to write my answers on the page. After about 15 minutes, Ms. Villavicencio asked loudly, "Would anyone be willing to share their answers to the class?"

I know myself very well. I never want to be called upon, so, I did what I usually do, and I looked away from my teacher's direction when I felt that she was possibly heading towards me or potentially looking at me.

Who ... ul For?
Year "2000"
COLLEGE
EMERGENCY

Of course, I didn't want to share my answers with the class. I may be opinionated but I usually kept my thoughts to myself. I didn't want to waste my energy on anything that doesn't concern me. I didn't feel the need to show off my intelligence because I already know that I'm intelligent, and if I knew that, then I'm pretty sure that my teacher and my classmates did too.

But alas, as my luck would have it, I always end up being chosen to present because I never protest. I do what I got to do because I ought to. Ms. Villavicencio continued, "Okay Arabella, why don't you present your answers to the class?"

Of course I felt shy, but being shy was not enough reason for me to refuse my teacher's request because I deeply cared for my teacher and I didn't want to do or say anything that could possibly offend her. It's the least that I could do for such a hard-working 'second mom' -- as she likes to refer to herself.

With all my courage and with all my might, I stood up from my seat and I read my answers to the entire class:

"I am grateful for my mom.
When we used to live in the Philippines, my mom used to be a computer engineer.
When we immigrated to Canada in the year 2000, my mom went back to college and became a laboratory assistant.
What does she do exactly?
Well, she takes people's blood … among other things.
Her job allows doctors to figure out how they can help their patients better by knowing exactly what ails them.
Actually, my mom is considered as a 'frontliner' too, and her work is super important for the community, so she takes her job very seriously.
I am most definitely proud of her because she's someone who takes the time to get to know a little bit about every single patient that she pokes with her needles.

FRONTLINER
I love you, Mom.
12:00 AM

She cares so deeply and sincerely about everyone around her, that she also ends up sharing a bit of herself to them, and likewise, they return the same courtesy towards her by sharing a bit of themselves too.
She's quite friendly and she gets along fine with everybody.
She's what's known as a 'social butterfly'.

Since I've been born, my mom's barely been home.
I never usually see her in the mornings.
I never usually see her in the afternoons.
I never usually see her at night too.
So, whenever I do see her, I make the most out of our conversations and our interactions.
Usually, I only see her between midnight and dawn, when sometimes I'd awaken from my deep sleep because I felt thirsty or hungry in the middle of the night.
Sometimes, I'd pop into my parent's bedroom to catch a glimpse of her while she's asleep and give her a quick kiss on her forehead and that was it.
I never did anything more than that besides whisper, "I love you, Mom," which she probably never heard as she tends to be in deep sleep too, and let's keep it that way because she never gets more than 5 hours of sleep every night.
She's a frontliner and she's my hero.

My mom always prioritizes our family's financial stability, which is the main reason why we never really get to see her often -- because she works extremely hard to be able to provide us with all our needs and wants.
When she was younger, she experienced poverty first-hand, and she always enlightens us that the reason we immigrated to Canada in the first place was to change our lives for the better.
So, whenever we tell her to "slow down" or "relax", she always reminds us that we must work hard while our minds and bodies are still young, strong, and healthy.
Simply put, my mom is a workaholic.

7 : 00 AM
7 : 00 PM
12 : 00 AM
7 : 00 AM
7 : 00 PM
12 : 00 AM

Even during her days off, she can't sit still, she's always on-the-go, and she
always has to keep herself busy.
Sometimes, there were days when it made me sad.
Sometimes, there were days when it made me lonely.
Sometimes, there were days when I just needed my mom to comfort me.
But this year, as I turn 12 years old, I have realized that my mom needs my
comfort more than I do.
I figured that if I felt sad for not seeing her a lot, then I'm sure that my mom
felt a thousand times sadder about not being able to see her family a lot.
I figured that if I felt lonely for not being with her a lot, then I'm sure that my
mom felt a thousand times lonelier about not being with us a lot.
I figured that if I needed my mom's comfort sometimes, I'm sure that my mom
needed our comfort a thousand times more for those days when she's feeling
some parts of her body aches, for those days when she's sick, and for those days
that she's feeling down.
So, I figured that instead of focusing only on myself and my feelings, I should
also put myself in my mom's shoes, and think about her, and consider her
situation, her thoughts, and her feelings because all this time, all she has ever
done is prioritize her family first and do what she thinks is best for her family.
Likewise, we strive to do the exact same for her -- we also have to make sure
that she feels that we put her first too.

My mom is inspirational and admirable.
Everyday, she leaves the house by 6 A.M. and she doesn't come home until 12:30
A.M, and that is around midnight.
That is some kind of true dedication and devotion to her family and her career.
Even though it pains me not to see her often, I know that what she's doing is
necessary for the greater good.

I am grateful for my mom because she sacrifices all of her time and she works
so hard to be able to put a roof above our heads.
She makes sure that we have a beautiful home to come back to.

DRINK

Even on her days off, she's always cleaning the house!
She can't even relax one bit because she says it's good exercise for her aging
bones.

I am grateful for my mom because she sacrifices all of her time and she works
so hard to be able to feed us delicious food.
She makes sure to buy a lot of ingredients so that our dad can cook us the best
tasting meals.
Even on her days off, she always takes us to the most delicious restaurants in
our city!
It makes me happy when she says, "Happy Tummy, Happy Life", because I
quite agree with that statement.

I am grateful for my mom because she sacrifices all of her time and she works
so hard to be able to give us the vacation of our dreams.
She makes sure to create a lot of beautiful memories with us and thankfully,
our Mom loves to travel too, so she always brings us to the best places.

I am from Edmonton, Alberta, Canada.
I love Canada as a whole because it's such a beautiful, diverse country, and if
you've ever been to Banff, Jasper, Vancouver, Toronto, or Montreal, among so
many other beautiful touristic sites in Canada -- you would know that its
beauty is just so mind-blowing and surreal!
Honestly, I could list so many heavenly places all over the world such as
Boracay Island, Philippines, and Palawan, Philippines, but the list would be too
long.

All I can say is that all of these were made possible because my mom constantly
pushed herself and continues to push herself to work extremely hard to be able
to give us a great life with the best experiences and the best memories of our
lives.

For all of the beautiful memories, experiences, people, and things in my life, I am and I will be forever grateful to my mom, and I will never ever get tired of making sure that she knows exactly how thankful I am to her and for her, how much I appreciate her, and how much I love her."

As soon as I finished reading my answers to the class, my peers started clapping. I felt relieved as soon as I looked up to see supportive faces around me. Some were even nodding to show their approval. I'm glad that everyone understood the message that I was trying my utmost best to convey to the class, and I'm sure that everyone found my piece relatable as I'm sure everyone also has a million and one reasons to be grateful to their own mothers.

"Thank you for sharing how grateful you are towards your mother, Arabella. That was truly a beautiful piece. Now, would anyone else like to share their piece as well? Who would like to go next? Raise your hand up!"

The rest of the day went by like a breeze, as they usually do in Ms. Villavicencio's class because mostly everyone liked her, especially when she brought Filipino snacks for us most of the time. Nobody ever went hungry in her class. We're always well-fed by her as she likes to lecture us that food allows people to enjoy each other's company. My teacher is such a beautiful soul!

The very next day, Ms. Villavicecio, addressed the entire class, "Well, I sure do hope that everyone completed their assignments. So, for Language Arts, in what ways do you suppose we can give back to those whom we are extremely grateful for? In other words, how can we show others that we are grateful towards them?"

What Are You Grateful For?
Lucky 1
Lucky 2

Arabella's best friend, Serafina, raised her hand to answer the question. As soon as Ms. Villavicencio gave her the go signal, Serafina stood up and exclaimed, "Ms. V, I'm grateful for my 2 Siberian cats, the Lucky Ones: Lucky One and Lucky Too. Yes, that's right, it's Lucky Too, not Lucky Two. They always keep me company and they always make me happy. In return, I show them my appreciation and my love by spending good quality time with them, and by buying them cute matching outfits! I'm always playing with them every chance I get because they are my responsibility and I enjoy them a lot."

"I'm glad to know that you have a heart of gold, my dear Serafina! Maybe you'll become a veterinarian one day."

"Oh, you bet, Ms. V! I most definitely will!" Serafina then sat down with a huge smile on her face, as the mere thought of Lucky 1 and Lucky Too made her happy.

Ms. Villavicencio turned around to face the entire class and asked once again, "Would anyone else be willing to share their answers to the class?"

Dead silence. Everyone looked away, and looked at anything but Ms. Villavicencio, sincerely hoping that they wouldn't get chosen because they didn't do their homework, and for those that did complete their homework -- well, there were those who were either too shy to share their answers, or those that could care less whether or not they were able to present their answers.

"Okay … then, let's ask Arabella to share her answers with the rest of the class."

"Anything for you, Ms. V." Slowly, Arabella stood up from her chair to read her answers to the class:

How do I show my mom that I am grateful to her and for her?
How can I show my mom that I am appreciative of her and make her feel that I do?
How can I make sure that my mom feels loved?
What can I do?
I don't have any money.
I can't buy her anything.
What should I do?

These are some of the questions that I had asked myself. First, I had to put myself in her shoes in order for me to be able to answer such questions and brainstorm what made my mom happy in the first place.

My mom is a simple person.
She's someone who thinks that the best things in life are free.
She always tells us that she does not need any material things.
Instead, what she loves is to invest in memories, experiences, travels, and adventures with us.

It makes my mom happy when she comes home to find my homework all done.
Whenever she comes home around midnight, she still sets aside the time to check my agenda and my finished homework before she goes to sleep.

It makes my mom happy when she comes home to find that I have prepared my lunch and my clothes for the next morning, so I am never rushing in the mornings.
After she comes home around midnight, she still sets aside the time to check that I have enough food for lunch and that my clothes are clean and ironed for the next day.

It makes my mom happy when she comes home to find that I have cleaned my room.
It's one less burden for her to think about and one less chore for her to do.

I mean, it's my room, my mess, my responsibility.
I shouldn't have to make my mom do it in the first place.

It makes my mom happy when I help my dad take care of my siblings.

For the next few chores, my siblings and I usually help each other with our
dad's guidance.

My mom loves surprises!
So, we tend to surprise her with good homemade meals.

It makes my mom happy to come home to a clean sink with the dishes all
washed, dried, and put away neatly.

It makes my mom happy to come home to clean floors with the floors all swept
and mopped.

It makes my mom happy to come home to a dust-free home.

It makes my mom happy to see all of our books and toys nicely tucked away in
their own bins.

It makes my mom happy to see picture and video messages of us throughout
the entire day and night.

It makes my mom happy when I help my dad read books with my siblings.

It makes my mom happy when my dad cooks delicious food for the family.

It makes my mom happy when we paint our nails together.

It makes my mom happy when we all just lay on the sofa bed and watch movie
marathons together, all snuggled up in the same blanket.

It makes my mom happy when we cook and eat together on her days off.

It makes my mom happy when we go on picnics when she's not working.

It makes my mom happy when we go camping in the mountains, near the lakes, and barbecue together during the holidays.

My mom is a Frontliner.
My dad taught us to make sure that my mom feels loved, appreciated, & cared for, for every single day that she has to work extremely hard for our family.
It's my dad who taught my siblings and I to treat each day as if it's Mother's Day.
He has lectured us countless times that it's not enough to tell someone how much they are loved, appreciated, and cared for.
He insists that love, care, and appreciation are feelings and emotions that must be shown and must be felt by the other person.
That's how special, valuable, and lovable my mom is to everyone.
We give her Mother's Day every day.
We appreciate her every moment of every day.
We care for her every moment of every day.
We honour her every moment of every day.
We love her every moment of every day.
We put her first.
Because she does the exact same thing for us.
She always puts us first.
She appreciates us every moment of every day.
She cares for us every moment of every day.
She honours us every moment of every day.
She loves us every moment of every day.

Our mom is a Frontliner.
For everyone in our family, we believe that our mom deserves to be treated like it's Mother's Day every day.

My mom came home at midnight from work, to find me sitting near the fireplace with my siblings and I reading together and doing homework too.

She came over to give us a very tight hug, "Hey mga anak, what are you still doing up? It's already way past your bedtime. You're going to be too exhausted and sleepy when you go to school tomorrow." The word 'mga anak' is a Tagalog term of endearment for the word 'my children'.

"We're so sorry, Nanay. I know that you've told us countless times that sleeping 8 hours a day is good for our developmental growth. You know how much we love to sleep too, but we also love the feeling of a finished task, so we don't have anything to worry about when we wake up." The word 'Nanay' is a Tagalog term of endearment for the word 'mom'.

"Well, what such task is keeping you all awake this long? Can I see?"

"Sure, Mom! It's about you actually. I hope you like it."

My mom exclaimed as she began to read, "I LOVE everything you all do for me, of course, I will LOVE it!"

Only a couple of minutes into it, she began to cry … A LOT. "This is truly so touching, anak. Come here and give me a hug! Why do you always do things or say things that melt my heart, darling? You and your siblings make me so proud to be your mother because you all make being a mother so easy. I know that I'm not a perfect mother, no one is, but you three children have such a kind heart and understanding mentality that you easily forgive Nanay for all of my shortcomings and flaws. I'm extremely happy, lucky, grateful, and blessed to have been blessed with such beautiful souls as my children and I wouldn't have it any other way. We're ONE family and we should always be the ones to forgive each other first. If we can be good to our friends or to strangers, then, it's imperative that we must be great to our family members first. We prioritize our family first. It's always family first."

We started crying together even more. When my mom mentioned, 'FAMILY FIRST', she's talking about our agreed-upon promise to one another that every single family member has to take on initiatives to be responsible for something, in order to make it easy for the rest of us because we work and function as a team. We always help each other out in ways that make the 'to-do list' at home easier to manage if everyone is working hard to complete tasks. Our dad taught us to do things properly the first time, so we'll never have to re-do the same job again because we've done it perfectly the first time. For example: my Dad cooks, I ensure that my siblings and I do our homework together and I help them with their homework, my younger brother washes the dishes, and my younger sister sweeps and mops the floor. Everyone has to work hard together to make everyone's lives easier, lighter, and happier.

"Nanay, I love you so much, and even during my lifetime, I can never repay you enough for everything that you have done for us. I'm also extremely happy, lucky, grateful, and blessed to have you as my Nanay." Nanay is the Tagalog term for "mother".

My mom smiled at me and kissed me on the cheek. My mom continued to read until she completed the whole essay.

"Anak, I'm so proud that you are such a great writer! I could feel your vulnerabilities and emotions coming out of the pages! Thank you so much for being so empathetic, so thoughtful, and so considerate of me. This is the most beautiful thing anyone can ever receive. This is enough happiness for me. Your love is enough to make me happy in my lifetime. I love you all so much!"

Arabella sat beside her mom and handed her mom a hand-made card that said, "Happy Mother's Day, Nanay! I love you so much with all of my heart!"

Arabella's mom exclaimed confusedly, "Arabella, it's not Mother's Day yet."

With a huge smile on her face, Arabella replied, "Mom! It's Mother's Day everyday, every time, everywhere!" They gave each other the tightest embrace.

ABOUT THE AUTHOR

Chantal Magracia is a Filipino-Canadian author, educator, entrepreneur, and philanthropist, who graduated with a Bachelor of Education degree from the University of Alberta, with a major in English and a minor in Social Studies.

She is an experienced teacher who has taught K-12 students, including adult learners since 2011 in Alberta, Canada.

Since elementary, she has always been extremely passionate about Character Education which encompasses values, principles, ethics, morals, virtues, good manners, right conduct, and proper etiquette. In her work, she is highly driven to model what empathy, compassion, kindness, acceptance, consideration, thoughtfulness, and understanding looks like in our daily lives. She's a dedicated and devoted life-long learner with great work ethics, who prefers to write children's books as her medium of choice, to share her learnings, reflections, epiphanies, wisdom, and growth regarding her constant pursuit of becoming the best version of herself simply by helping and uplifting others.

In 2020, she co-founded a non-profit organization known as "The Alberta Society of Islamic Fellowship" or "ASIF", and she serves as ASIF's very first President. Together with Heidi Parel, Mary Joe Aissa, Evelyn Serbout, Suzan Nihad, Mechil Templado, Maryam Elfeki, Myrna Al-Kassab, and Jelena Babic, they help the poor, the needy, and the vulnerable, both locally, provincially, nationally, and internationally.

THANK YOU SO MUCH FOR PURCHASING MY PASSION PROJECT!

www.ingramcontent.com/pod-product-compliance
Lightning Source LLC
Chambersburg PA
CBHW042138030726
47599CB00002B/524